Alfred's
ULTIMATE EASY PLAY-ALONG | GUITAR

THE BRITISH INVASION. 1964

Seven Beatles Songs That Started It All

DVD VIDEO™

The DVD contains detailed video lessons for every song in the book. It will play in a standard DVD player or in a computer with a DVD drive.

TNT² CUSTOM MIX

In addition to video lessons, the DVD contains our exclusive TNT 2 software that you can use to hear professional sound-alike recordings of every song in the book, alter the instrument and vocal mixes of the recordings for practice, loop playback, and change keys and tempos.

For installation, insert the DVD into a computer, double-click on **My Computer**, right-click on the CD drive icon, and select **Explore**. (Mac users can simply double-click the DVD icon that appears on the desktop.) Open the **"DVD-ROM Materials"** folder, then the **"TNT 2"** folder, and double-click on the installer file. Installation may take up to 15 minutes.

mp3

For your convenience, the included disc contains sound-alike and play-along MP3s of each song. These extras are in the **"DVD-ROM Materials"** folder—see the TNT 2 instructions at left to find that folder.

SYSTEM REQUIREMENTS

Windows
7, Vista, XP
1.8 GHz processor or faster
2 GB hard drive space, 2 GB RAM minimum
Speakers or headphones
Internet access required for updates

Macintosh
OS 10.4 and higher (Intel only)
2 GB hard drive space, 2 GB RAM minimum
Speakers or headphones
Internet access required for updates

Alfred

Produced by
Alfred Music Publishing Co., Inc.
P.O. Box 10003
Van Nuys, CA 91410-0003
alfred.com

Printed in USA.

ISBN-10: 0-7390-9142-5 (Book & DVD)
ISBN-13: 978-0-7390-9142-5 (Book & DVD)

Cover photos: Höfner Violin Bass courtesy of KARL HÖFNER GmbH & Co. KG • Gibson J-160E courtesy of Gibson Musical Instruments • Gretsch G6128T-GH George Harrison Signature Duo Jet courtesy of Fred W. Gretsch Enterprises, Ltd. • Gretsch Country Gentleman courtesy of Fred W. Gretsch Enterprises, Ltd.

Recordings and video produced at Alfie Road Studios by John Allen and Aaron Stang

Contents*

* To access sound-alike and play-along MP3s and the TNT 2 software that lets you alter the audio, see pg. 1.

DO YOU WANT TO KNOW A SECRET

Words and Music by
JOHN LENNON and PAUL McCARTNEY

Do You Want to Know a Secret - 3 - 1

FROM ME TO YOU

Words and Music by
JOHN LENNON and PAUL McCARTNEY

*Guitar chord grids indicate fingerings for the rhythm slash guitar.
Notated guitar parts often use other voicings shown in the TAB.
**Play all octave figures with pick and fingers.

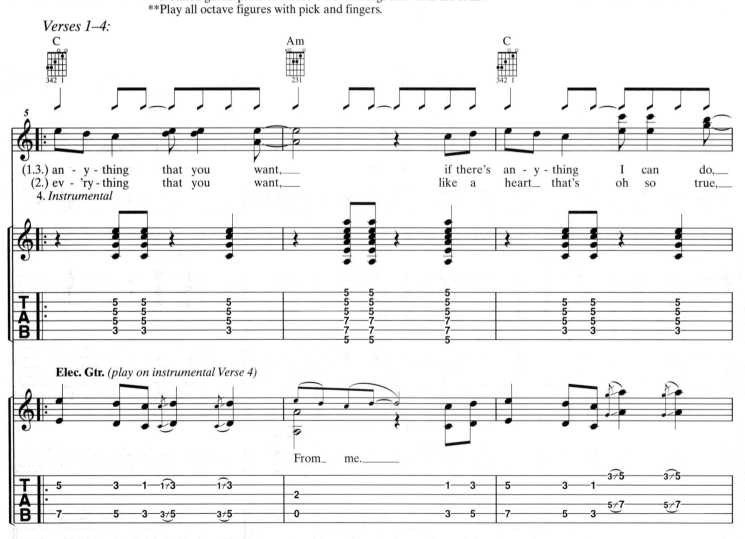

From Me to You - 4 - 1

Bridge:

arms that long to hold___ you and keep you by my

side. I've got lips that long to kiss___ you and

keep you sat - is - fied, ooo. 3. If there's fied, ooo. If there's

*Play cue-size notes on repeat.

Verse 5:

I WANNA BE YOUR MAN

Words and Music by
JOHN LENNON and PAUL McCARTNEY

*Guitar chord grids indicate fingerings for the rhythm slash guitar.
Notated guitar parts often use other voicings shown in the TAB.

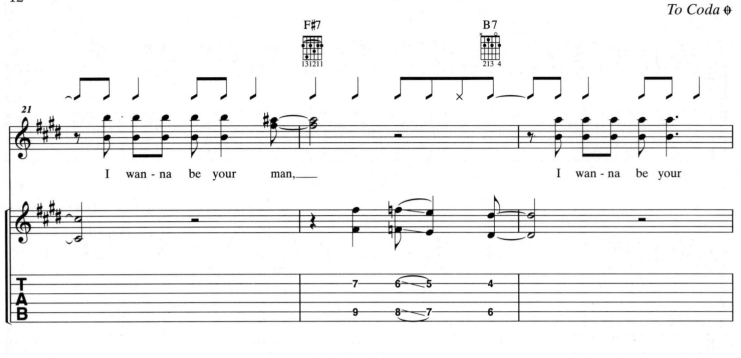

I wan-na be your man,___ I wan-na be your

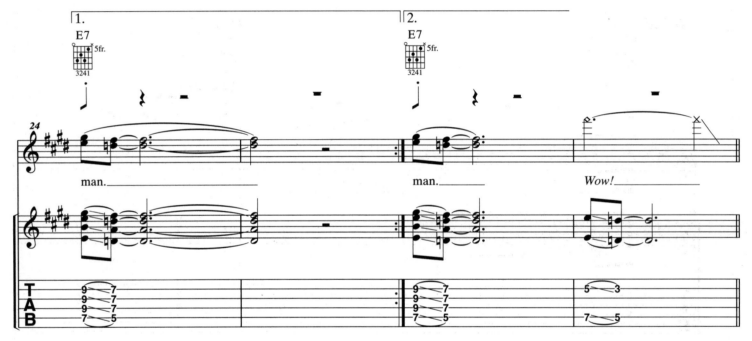

man.___ man.___ *Wow!*___

Guitar Solo:

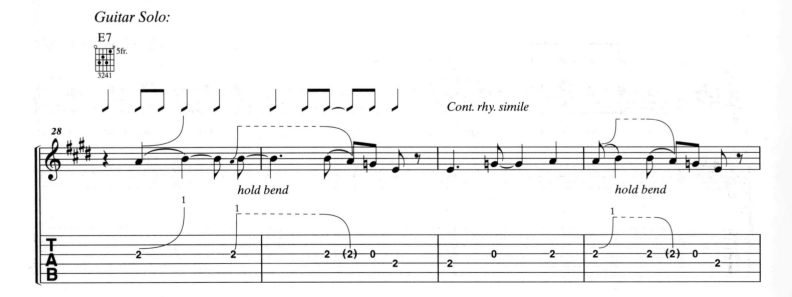

I SAW HER STANDING THERE

Moderately fast ♩ = 160

Words and Music by
JOHN LENNON and PAUL McCARTNEY

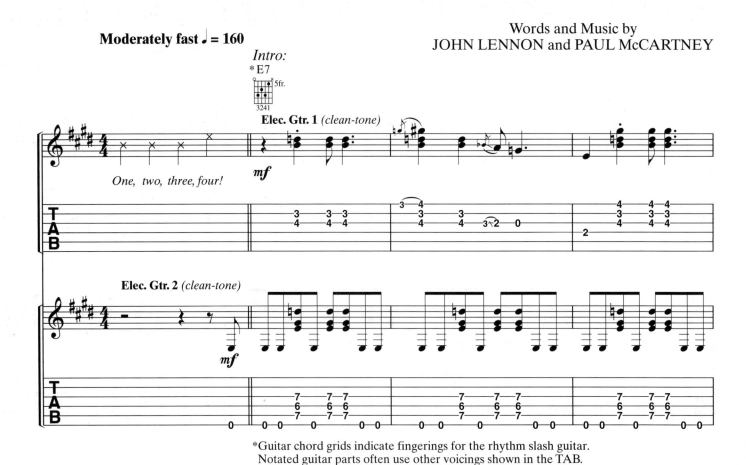

*Guitar chord grids indicate fingerings for the rhythm slash guitar.
Notated guitar parts often use other voicings shown in the TAB.

Verses 1 & 2:

1. Well, she was just___ sev-en-teen,___ you know what I___ mean..
2. *See additional lyrics*

I Saw Her Standing There - 7 - 1

Verses 3 & 4:

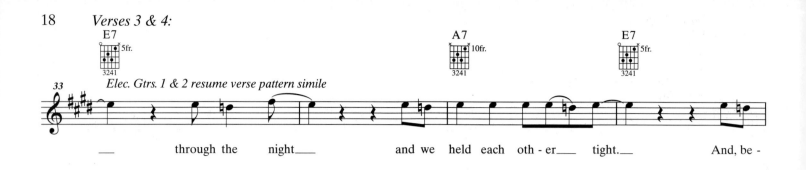

Elec. Gtrs. 1 & 2 resume verse pattern simile

_____ through the night_____ and we held each oth - er_____ tight._____ And, be -

fore too long, I fell in love_____ with her._____ Now,

Elec. Gtr. 1

w/Rhy. Fig. 1 (Elec. Gtr. 1) cont. simile

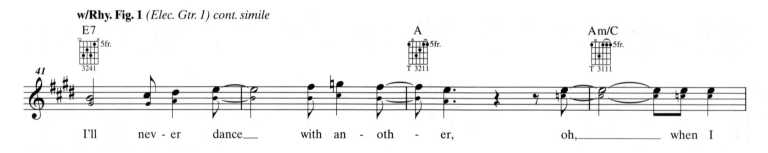

I'll nev - er dance_____ with an - oth - er, oh,_____ when I

To Coda ⊕

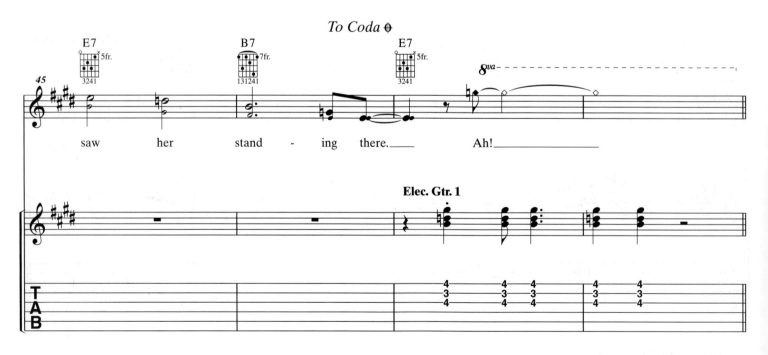

saw her stand - ing there._____ Ah!_____

Elec. Gtr. 1

Guitar Solo:

⊕ Coda

Verse 2:
Well, she looked at me and I, I could see
That, before too long, I'd fall in love with her.
She wouldn't dance with another, oh,
When I saw her standing there.
(To Bridge:)

MISERY

Words and Music by
JOHN LENNON and PAUL McCARTNEY

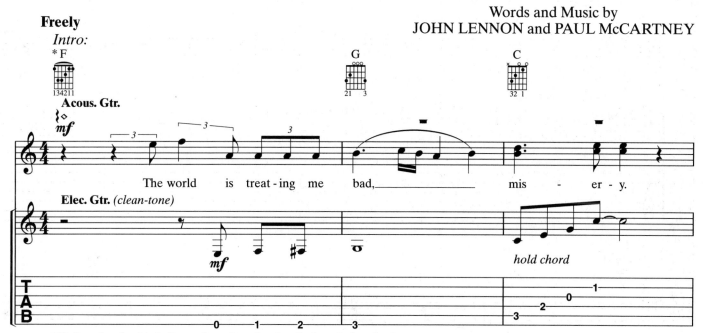

*Guitar chord grids indicate fingerings for the rhythm slash guitar.
Notated guitar parts often use other voicings shown in the TAB.

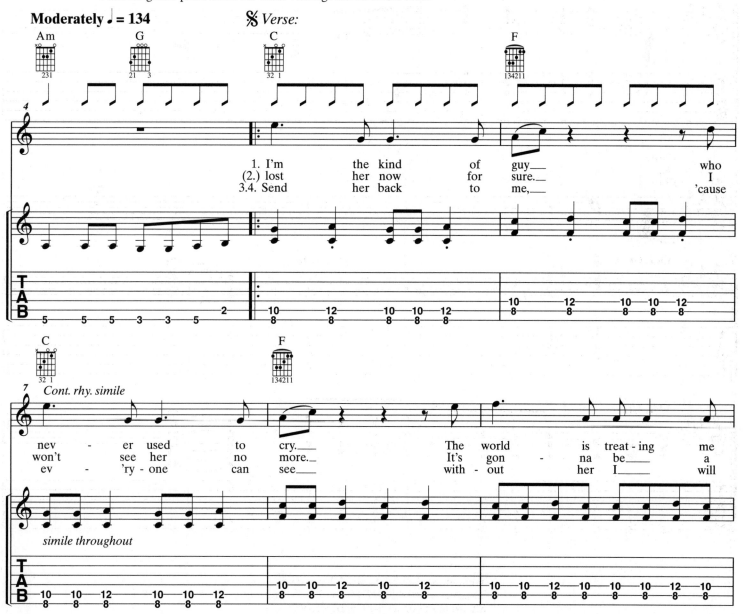

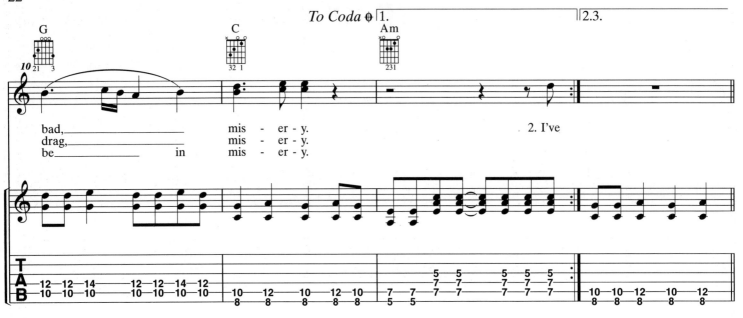

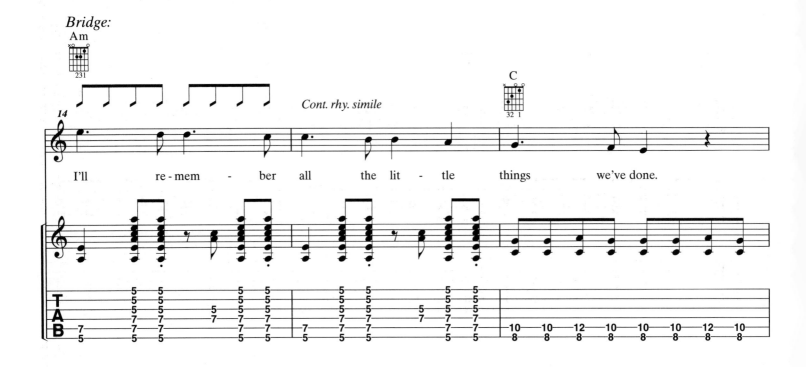

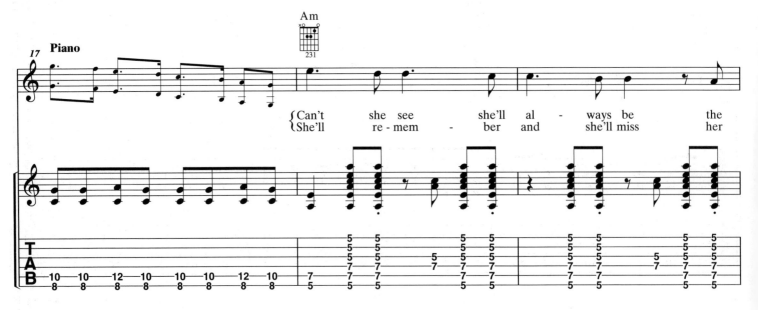

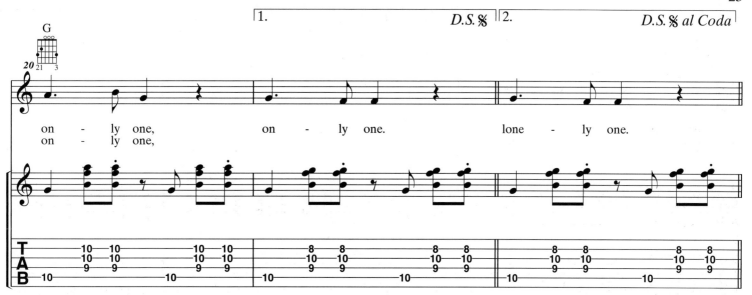

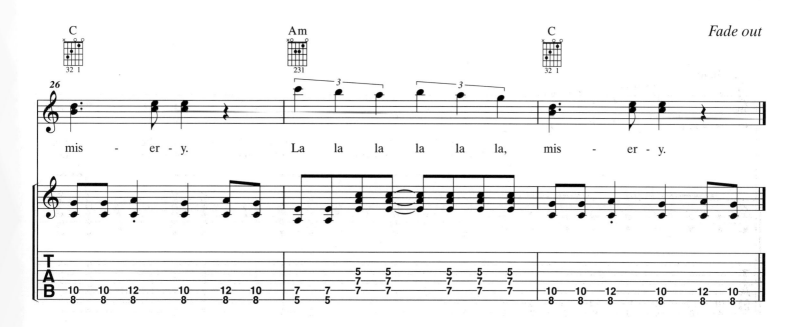

SHE LOVES YOU

Words and Music by
JOHN LENNON and PAUL McCARTNEY

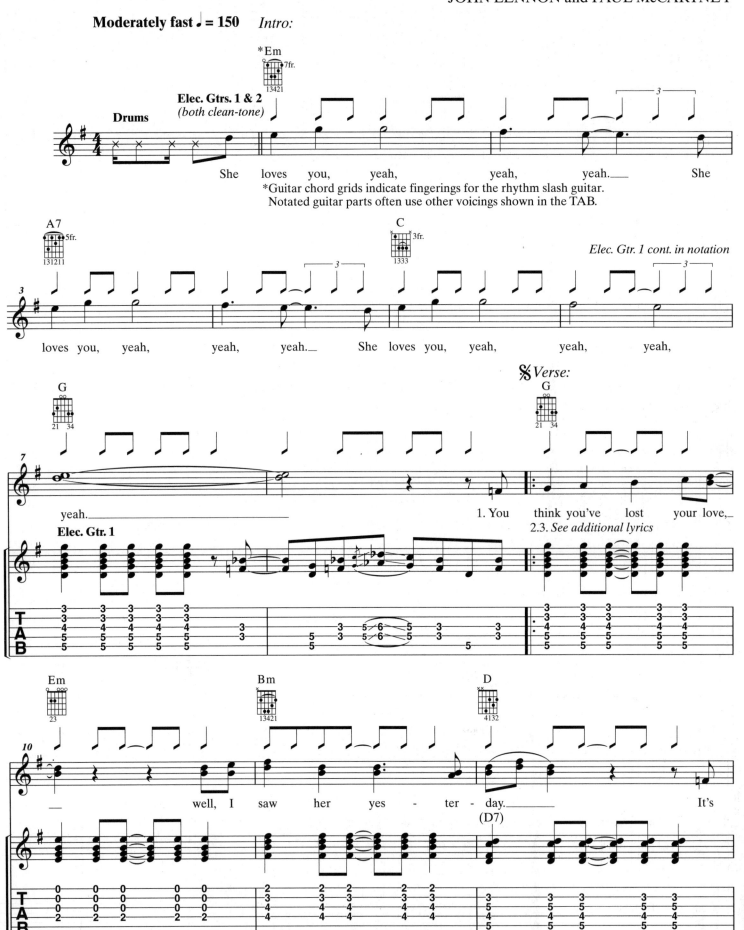

*Guitar chord grids indicate fingerings for the rhythm slash guitar.
Notated guitar parts often use other voicings shown in the TAB.

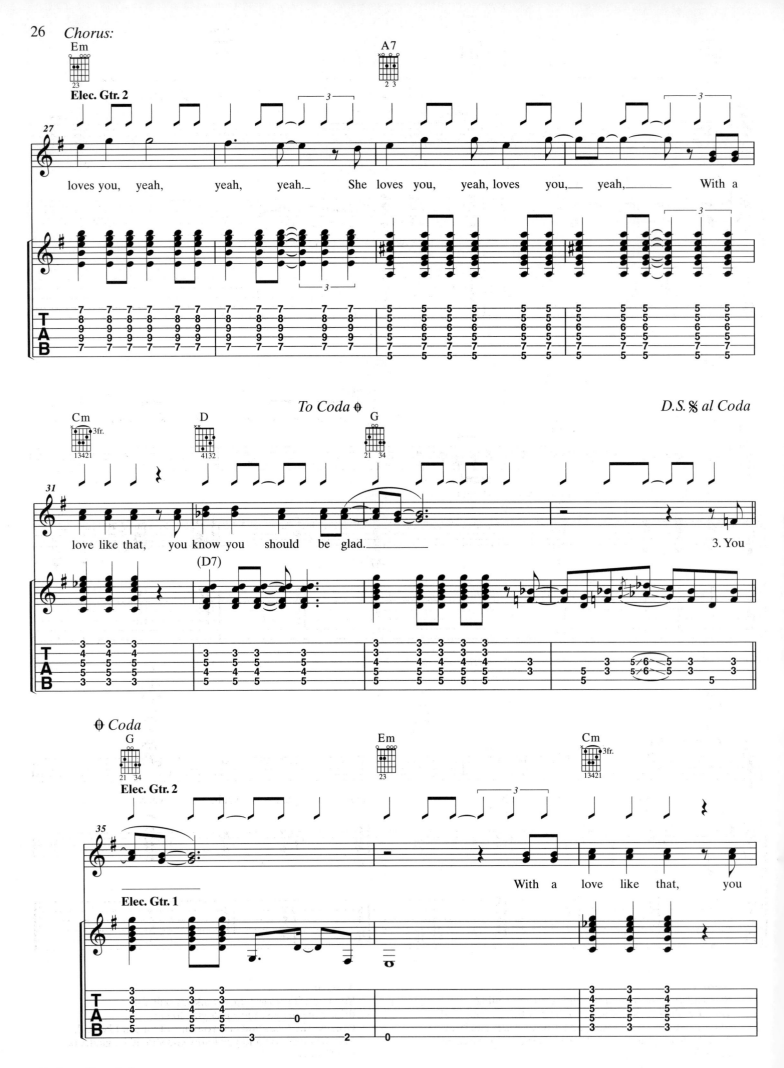

Verse 2:
She said you hurt her so she almost lost her mind.
But now she says she knows you're not the hurting kind.
She said she loves you and you know that can't be bad.
Yes, she loves you and you know you should be glad, oo.
(To Chorus:)

Verse 3:
You know it's up to you, I think it's only fair.
Pride can hurt you too, apologize to her.
Because she loves you and you know that can't be bad.
Yes, she loves you and you know you should be glad, oo.
(To Chorus:)

THERE'S A PLACE

Moderately fast ♩ = 140

Words and Music by
JOHN LENNON and PAUL McCARTNEY

*Guitar chord grids indicate fingerings for the rhythm slash guitar. Notated guitar parts often use other voicings shown in the TAB.

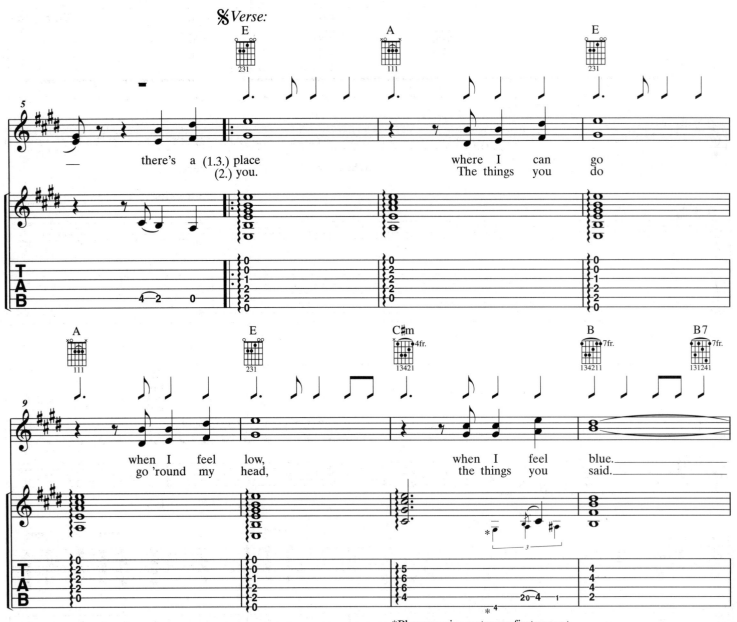

*Play cue-size notes on first repeat.

TABLATURE EXPLANATION
TAB illustrates the six strings of the guitar.
Notes and chords are indicated by the placement of fret numbers on each string.

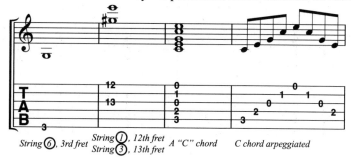

String ⑥, 3rd fret   *String ①, 12th fret*   *A "C" chord*   *C chord arpeggiated*
                     String ③, 13th fret

BENDING NOTES

Half Step:
Play the note and bend string one half step (one fret).

Whole Step:
Play the note and bend string one whole step (two frets).

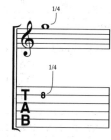

Slight Bend/ Quarter-Tone Bend:
Play the note and bend string sharp.

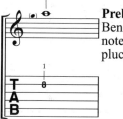

Prebend (Ghost Bend):
Bend to the specified note before the string is plucked.

Prebend and Release:
Play the already-bent string, then immediately drop it down to the fretted note.

Unison Bends:
Play both notes and immediately bend the lower note to the same pitch as the higher note.

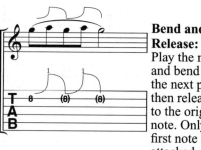

Bend and Release:
Play the note and bend to the next pitch, then release to the original note. Only the first note is attacked.

Bends Involving More Than One String:
Play the note and bend the string while playing an additional note on another string. Upon release, relieve the pressure from the additional note allowing the original note to sound alone.

Bends Involving Stationary Notes:
Play both notes and immediately bend the lower note up to pitch. Return as indicated.

ARTICULATIONS

Hammer On:
Play the lower note, then "hammer" your finger to the higher note. Only the first note is plucked.

Pull Off:
Play the higher note with your first finger already in position on the lower note. Pull your finger off the first note with a strong downward motion that plucks the string—sounding the lower note.

Legato Slide:
Play the first note and, keeping pressure applied on the string, slide up to the second note. The diagonal line shows that it is a slide and not a hammer-on or a pull-off.

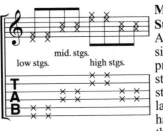

Muted Strings:
A percussive sound is produced by striking the strings while laying the fret hand across them.

Palm Mute:
The notes are muted (muffled) by placing the palm of the pick hand lightly on the strings, just in front of the bridge.

HARMONICS

Natural Harmonic:
A finger of the fret hand lightly touches the string at the note indicated in the TAB and is plucked by the pick producing a bell-like sound called a harmonic.

RHYTHM SLASHES

Strum Marks/ Rhythm Slashes:
Strum with the indicated rhythm pattern. Strum marks can be located above the staff or within the staff.

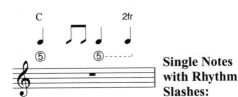

Single Notes with Rhythm Slashes:
Sometimes single notes are incorporated into a strum pattern. The circled number below is the string and the fret number is above.

Artificial Harmonic:
Fret the note at the first TAB number, lightly touch the string at the fret indicated in parens (usually 12 frets higher than the fretted note), then pluck the string with an available finger or your pick.

TREMOLO BAR

Specified Interval:
The pitch of a note or chord is lowered to the specified interval and then return as indicated. The action of the tremolo bar is graphically represented by the peaks and valleys of the diagram.

Unspecified Interval:
The pitch of a note or chord is lowered, usually very dramatically, until the pitch of the string becomes indeterminate.

PICK DIRECTION

Downstrokes and Upstrokes:
The downstroke is indicated with this symbol (⊓) and the upstroke is indicated with this (∨).